MW01268788

# I'll Meet You
# on the
# Other Side

## Mary Rita WaldschmidtBauck

Other Books by Mary

*I am but a Stranger here, Heaven is my Home*

Published through LuLu.com

Find more books by Mary on the World Wide Web www.LuLu.com Search: Mary Bauck

ISBN: 978-0-9895607-1-9

This book is dedicated to
My dear friend Florida TongolBanawa
who touched my heart and my soul
by the way she lived her life
April 10, 1949 – May 11, 2016

# TABLE OF CONTENTS

## Foreword

Several of my poems and prayers are about me having a hard time getting through the day. I ask God for His help. Perhaps you have had days like this. No matter how we feel, we can let God know our problems and He will help us. On better days we should tell Him about the good things happening in our lives and thank Him for His blessings.

I'd like to go back in time to when I first met Florida. We were both members of Victorious Missionaries – a spiritual support group for people who have chronic illness or disease. The main headquarters is in Belleville, Illinois, at Our Lady of the Snows. There are several small groups around the United States.

I wrote a book and made an audio tape called "I am but a Stranger here, Heaven is My Home." I sent a copy of the book and CD to the main group and to each smaller group. I first encountered Florida after she read my book. She called me and said how much she enjoyed my book. She said, "You can be my writing instructor." Later I laughed when I found out what an excellent writer she was. She wrote many poems, prayers, and even a story about her life called, "Profile of Courage." A lot of her writings were published in our "Up Lift" quarterly newsletter.

From the first time Florida called me, we were instant friends. There are some people in life that you meet and it is as though you have known them all of your life. Our illnesses and love of God cemented our relationship. She inspired me and everyone she met with her upbeat attitude, smile, and ray of sunshine. On May 11, 2016 Florida passed. Now she is healthy and doesn't need her wheelchair any more.

The first three poems of this collection I sent to Florida. She said I should send them to Victorious Missionaries so they could put them in our quarterly newsletter. I did – the next newsletter had a picture of her with her obituary. Alongside of that was my poem, "My Special Friend Florida."

Someone asked if my description of Heaven is a dream, a vision, or my imagination. It is none of those. I just know what it is like. God helped me write this book – He inspired me, I was only his writing instrument.

I highly recommend journaling. You need to get your feelings out. Writing them down can help you cope with a lot of things going on in your life. This book contains poems about Heaven, my struggles with each day, and my hope of God waiting to take me to Heaven - because as much as I want to be with God and all of my loved ones, I still want more time to get things done while on earth. I also want God to continue to inspire me in the hopes of bringing people closer to God and putting their worries aside as they find out what Heaven is like.

God Bless You and Hold You,
Mary Rita WaldschmidtBauck

## Standing at Death's Doorway

On February seventeenth and eighteenth, 2016, I felt so bad that I didn't think I would be around much longer. On the seventeenth, I wrote a poem, "Standing at Death's Doorway." About a week later, my despair and uneasiness vanished. What I find interesting is that I have kept journals for years and after writing about half of this book, I read one journal from 1985 that stated, "I don't think I will be around much longer." That was thirty-two years ago and I'm still here. I'm glad about that - it will be interesting to see what the Lord has in store for me.

## Standing at Death's Doorway

I'm standing at death's doorway
  Afraid to take a peek inside,
To leave all I know behind me
  And discover what's on the other side.

I know I have had trials and tribulations
  While here on earth I stood,
Yet I'm afraid to take that step
  I'd rather stay here if I could.

I hear of promises before me
  And know there's no reason for fears,
Yet not knowing what it's like
  And what I leave behind causes all the tears.

The pain some days is unbearable,
  But I'm promised pain will be all gone.

And what a glorious meeting with loved ones;
  I must have faith and courage to travel to the place
beyond.

## My Special Friend Florida

Around the twenty-fourth of February, I received a call
from my friend Florida. She told me she had been receiving
chemotherapy for several weeks, as she had cancer. The
treatments were very hard on her. She suffered a lot in her
life already, due to rheumatoid arthritis since 1975. After
talking to her, I wrote my second poem, "My Special
Friend Florida." Little did I know that in a few short
months she would be in Heaven.

## My Special Friend Florida

God sent to me a special friend
  We can be ourselves, not needing to pretend.
We talk about our God whom we both love so,
  Why He put us together we don't really know.
We are able to talk and share our pain,
  We are friends forever and that won't change.
Even after we've gone to Heaven above
  We will always share His divine love.

We both have suffered, but we don't mind.
  We know God has a plan for us at this time.
And some day when we meet in God's kingdom of Love
  We will laugh and shout from up above.

We will walk thru the gardens with flowers all around,

And listen to all the joyful sounds
Of the beautiful birds as they fly thru the air,
  And know the reason for all our prayers.

To be one with Him it is hard to explain,
  Like the rainbow in the sky after a summer rain.
And seeing our loved ones that before us went,
  They are waiting for the day when we will be sent.

What a joyous reunion it will be
  As we see each other – you and me.
We will hug and laugh – what a special time
  It's hard to imagine God is so kind.

That He put both of us together on earth below
  So we could talk and pray until it is time to go
To the beautiful Heaven where we will be free,
  Young, and in good health for eternity.

**I'll Meet You on the Other Side**

My third poem, "I'll Meet You on the Other Side" was
written before Florida died. Since I wrote that poem I have
given it to people who have lost a loved one and many say
they feel it is their loved one speaking to them from
Heaven.

**I'll Meet You on the Other Side**

I'll meet you on the other side.
  My Guardian Angel was my guide.
Oh what a joyful day it will be

When you are standing next to me.

The beauty of Heaven is a sight to behold.
  You can't imagine even if you are told.
The beauty of the Heavenly Hosts
  Is what impressed me the most.

My family all came to see me;
  What a precious sight to see.
And all my friends who went ahead
  Were waiting here just like they said.
All my pets, both large and small
  Were waiting there beside the wall
Of the beautiful city all diamonds and gold -
  What a sight it was to behold.

You could never imagine what awaits thee.
  It far surpassed what I thought it would be.
The birds in the air and the sky so blue…
  Wait until you see what awaits you.

And the clouds – I never imagined they would be there.
  It's kind of like an answered prayer.
You know how I loved them on earth below.
  There are so many surprises for you to know.

I'm here waiting for you on the other side.
  I have so much to show you and I'll be your guide.
You don't have to rush to Heaven's door.
  Eternity awaits you – you couldn't ask for more.

## Do You Hear Me Lord?

Do you hear me Lord? I keep calling.
  I need to get thru a few more days
To get things taken care of here
  Before to Heaven I raise.

I am looking forward, Lord,
  To the day when we meet face to face.
But please allow me some more time
  To make sure all I have is in its place.

The days get harder and harder to bear.
  I have so little time
Before you take me home with you
  And unlock the chains that bind.

I know I shouldn't worry, Lord,
  About the things I leave behind.
But I can't help it Lord, I want things in order.
  I hope that you don't mind.

It's so hard, Lord, because I don't feel well,
  And so I'm slow at what needs to be done.
Have pity on me, Lord, and help me thru the day
  To get things completed before death has won.

Do you hear me, Lord? I don't really know.
  My life is slipping fast.
And it's oh so hard to do all the things
  And finish each and every task.

I love you Lord – You know I do.
  So be patient with me now.
I need more time, more time I say,
  And I hope my request you will allow.

**Arrival at the Golden Gates**

May 11, 2016, was a very special day. That's the day that
Florida arrived at the Kingdom of God. The gates opened
wide and Florida seemed to effortlessly float through.
There were angels around and God Himself was there to
greet her. His arms opened to embrace His loved one and
welcome her home. He told her how proud He was of her
and the way she lived her life. He said He was sorry that
she had to suffer so much over the years but the way she
carried herself through life was an inspiration to all.

After God's warm embrace, He showed her around Heaven
and she was in such awe of its beauty, words could scarcely
describe it. She saw her parents and other family and
friends that went before her. They were young and in good
health as Florida is now. She could walk, she could run,
and she jumped in the air. It was so nice to have a good
body.

As God showed her around, angels walked alongside.
Florida was so full of questions about this wonderful place
that she had heard about for years and to actually be here –
WOW!! It was so overwhelming. There were mansions all
around and she was able to select the one she loved best.
She took her shoes and socks off and ran through the
luscious grass as it tickled her toes. There was a blue

stream that she sat by and soaked her feet in. Birds were all around chirping melodies. Butterflies fluttered about the gorgeous flowers. One of her cats came and sat beside her and she petted it and it purred. Florida was so happy to be in God's Kingdom of Love.

I was privileged to know Florida. After reading my book, "I am but a Stranger here, Heaven is my Home," she called to thank me and an instant friendship began. No matter what life held for her – whether in joy or in pain, she praised God and cheered others up. Her face radiated a total love and rays of sunshine came from her. She served God well over the years despite her pain – I was going to say "limitations," due to her arthritis, but Florida knew no limitations. She was an inspiration to everyone she touched. Knowing her and what she has gone through in her life connected us. I don't have the words to describe the love in my heart for her. She loved life, her family and friends, but most of all she loved God.

And so dear friend, even though I have shed many tears for my loss, I am so happy for you. Being with God is a dream come true and some day when it's my turn, I know you will greet me. In an earlier poem, I wrote about you and said, "What a glorious reunion it will be. We will hug and laugh and we both will be free and young and in good health." Goodbye, dear friend, until we meet in God's Kingdom of Love.

## Dear Friend

Dear Friend,

The last time you called me, was that to say good-bye? You told me in the middle of the night you were waiting for God to take you home.

You were in a wheelchair for a number of years crippled by rheumatoid arthritis and then you got cancer. The chemotherapy was hard on you. Now that you have gone to live with God, it's a joyous time.

When I first heard you had died, I was devastated. I cried and cried but then I remembered where you are at - in Heaven and I can celebrate your new life, a life without your wheelchair and without pain. I am so happy for you. I look forward to the day when we finally meet.

You were very talented and had a way with words. You wrote several poems and prayers and they were published in our Up Lift newsletter. They were an inspiration to others, just as your life was an inspiration.

I thank God for letting me know such a wonderful person. You have left footprints on my heart.

By Mary Rita Bauck in memory of my friend Florida

## Coming to the End of the Line

I'm coming to the end of the line.
  It soon will be over and then I will find
What's on the other side and be truly alive.

My steps get slower as each painful step I take,
  Wishing the doctors could fix me for my sake.
I don't want to leave, there's too much here I love.
  I ask God the Father and Son above

To leave me here for a few more years,
  There is so much left I want to do -
To write words of comfort to see others through.

I want to spend time with family and friends.
  I know they will be beside me until the end.
Oh, I'm going to miss them when it is time to go.
  The time is getting shorter and shorter I know.

In the meantime I try not to complain.
  I blame it on the cold weather or rain.
Others don't need to know the heavy cross I carry.
  They will find out soon enough when my body is buried.

Then they can rejoice as to Heaven I go,
  I will be able to move fast, not slow.
I will be with my God and happy I will be.
  Feeling good, like an eagle I will soar free.

## Another Day

God granted me another day
To work, laugh and play.

I'm sitting outside.
I just fed my cats and with full bellies
They chase each other around.

Shiloh, the smallest and daintiest of the four
Runs up so high in the tree.

Her brother, Fluffy, tries not to be out done,
He races up the tree behind her.
But he can't go as high as Shiloh.

I wonder how they will get down,
But it's no problem, as I soon see.
Sometimes it's face first, other times the rear -

I have to remember to enjoy the little things in life and not
worry every minute.

## Help Me Lord

Help me to be brave, Lord.
  Help me to be strong.
Help me to carry my cross
  As you carried yours.

You stumbled and fell.
  Lord I stumble too.
Once I've fallen
  It's hard to get up again.

I know I have to.
  I know I can't give in,
But sometimes it feels
  Like I have to.

I know I should be braver,
  I know I should be strong.
Yet sometimes I feel like staying in bed
  And not getting up at all.

Please help me, Lord.
  Help me get through another day,
I can't do it on my own.
  I really, really need You.

Please give me Your strength, O Lord,
  Give me Your Courage,
Lift me up from the despair I feel,
  Lead me to someone I can confide in.

Someone who will help hold me together
  As I grow in my faith and trust in You.
And see the rainbow in the sky
  That comes after a storm
Then the sun shines and the
  world is a brighter place

I felt hopeless but with the new day,

  Your help and my trust in You, I will survive.
I realize I may still have hard days but I will overcome

them.

   You have shown me I can go on, There is hope in my heart,
And I know I can go on as you are always with me.

**From the Pages of my Journal**

In the pages of my journal after my Mother died in May of 1993, I would start my journals with, "Dear Mom." I had a wonderful mother and I thank God for that. I took her death hard – we thought so much alike and often knew what the other person was going to say before they actually spoke.

Dear Mom,

   I have a feeling that it won't be long now until I see your smiling face. What a smile you had; it seemed to light up the whole room.

   And the conversations we had – it was so nice to talk to you. Sometimes we would change the subject and we both would say the same thing – like stereo. It had nothing to do with what we previously were talking about – our minds just seemed to be on the same wave length.

   It has been twenty-three years since you left this earthly dwelling and went to live with God, the angels, and all of your loved ones.

   I never asked you if you and your mother had the same connection we had. I have a feeling that you did. She had your smile and your sense of humor. Grandma Mary liked cats like I do.

Your Mom lived in Milwaukee and you and the rest of your family lived in Detroit. In 1952, I was nine years old and my brother, Paul, was thirteen and we traveled by bus to see your Mom, since she was sick with heart problems. The last trip we made to see her, Paul stayed home and I went with you.

The night before Grandma Mary went to the hospital for the last time, you went out with your sister. Grandma and I had a real nice time. We went through her jewelry box and she gave me some pieces of her jewelry. I really enjoyed our time alone.

The next day, she went to the hospital. She was in there for several days before she died. In those days they didn't let children into the hospital.

Every day you fixed me a box of bread crumbs and crackers to feed the ducks while you and Aunt Harriet visited Grandma. There was a man-made lake that had a lot of ducks in it. When the ducks saw me coming, they would swim up and gather around me on the grass while I fed them. I really enjoyed my time with the ducks, but then a man kept watching me so you brought me into the hospital. I got to go to the room where my Grandma was, but I had to stay in the hall. All I could do was smile and wave at her from the doorway. I wanted so bad to hug her and give her a kiss but I wasn't allowed in the room. When I look back on it now, I wish I hadn't been so obedient and would have ran up to her and put my arms around her. That's the first thing I will do when I see her in Heaven.'

NOTE: I have written in a journal a lot over the years and I have found that it helps getting your feelings down on paper.

## Take it Slow

I was talking to a writer friend and we got into a discussion about so many young adults committing suicide. She said I have a way with words and I should write something to let people know if they wait twenty-four hours things would look better. After I got off the phone, I looked at a picture of Jesus and said, "What do you think?" "Take it Slow," was my answer. I only wrote two stanzas before my sister came in and so I stopped – for that was all He wanted me to say.

## Take it Slow

　　The words I write are not from me, they come from God who is so near. I am only the instrument that fills the page with what God wants you to hear. There is help for you, just relax and take it slow.

You may be hurting and
　don't know which way to go.
　That will all change,
There are better days ahead.
God is telling you through these words,
Tomorrow will be better but
You have to take it slow.

Sometimes it is hard to believe.
Tomorrow will change.
The sun will shine.
Have hope and take it slow.

## Come to Me

"Come to Me" is God calling to us. I especially like the part where He says, "Close your eyes, imagine My arms around you, I care for you, I love you, No one can take that away from you, you are VERY SPECIAL.."

## Come to Me

When you are tired and weary
  come to Me.
My arms are always open wide.
  I will wrap My arms around you –
See how you feel –
  The warmth from My arms gives you comfort.

It doesn't matter what is going on in your life –
  You can be joyful or sad.
You can come to Me any time – day or night.
  All you have to do is call Me.

Close your eyes and imagine My arms around you,
  I care for you
    I love you
      No one can take that away from you
        You are VERY SPECIAL.

Talk to Me – tell Me how you feel.
  Remember, I am always beside you,
    In you
      Around you
I am with every breath you take.

If you have done something wrong,
  Know that I will forgive you
If you ask and if you are sincere.

If you are proud of something you did,
  Tell Me that too. I am happy for you.

Talk to Me any time of the day,
  Tell Me what is going on in your life –
You can share everything with Me.

Most importantly know that
  I WILL ALWAYS, ALWAYS LOVE YOU.

## Time Is Running Out

Time is Running Out talks about a clock going backwards.
I feel we have a limited amount of time on earth so the
clock is going backwards.

## Time is Running Out

Tick tock, tick tock The clock is moving backwards and it
won't stop.
Time is running out – there's not much time

Until I journey to Heaven.
Then things will all be fine.

No more pain and no more strife
Soon it will be the end of my life -
The life as I know it here below.
God is calling and soon I must go.

I really don't want to leave
My family and my friends,
But as we all know
Our life here on earth will end.

I'll meet my friend, Florida.
We will meet face to face.
Our arms will go around each other
In a warm embrace.

We never met each other on earth below.
We emailed and called each other -
That's how our friendship did grow.
And soon I will be with her in Heaven above,
I will enter into God's kingdom of Love.

## Lord, Give Me Strength

Please give me your strength, O Lord.
  Give me Your courage,
Lift me up from the despair I feel.
  Lead me to someone who will listen.

Someone who will help hold me together

As I grow in my faith and trust in You,
And see the rainbow in the sky
  That comes after a storm.
Then the sun shines and the world
  Is a brighter place.

I felt hopeless, but with the new day
  And my trust in You,
I know I can go on.
  I know I can survive.

There is hope in my heart
  Because I believe You
Will be beside me,
  And You will carry me if necessary.

## Pray for Me

Pray for me so I can carry my cross bravely,
  Pray for me so I don't stop and complain.
There are so many people out there that are worse off than
me,
  I have to keep reminding myself of this as I hurt with each
step I take.

I have a walker and many times I'm bent over as each
  Painful step I take.
It would be so easy to say
  "That's it, I quit. I won't try anymore."
It would be so easy to surrender
  And not get out of bed any more.
It's very tempting – I could eliminate some of the pain,

But Jesus carried His cross for me,
Who am I to give up and say, "No more?
  I can't take it Lord, it's much too hard.
But you never said it would be easy."

Ever since I was a little girl
  I wanted to be a martyr or a saint –
That's a big laugh – I have sinned so much over the years.
  As time has passed by I said or did something
That hurt people. I didn't do it intentionally,
  But none the less – I did and I am sorry.

Forgive me Lord, forgive me.
  What more can I say or do?
When others ask if they can help me
  As the pain they see in everything I do.
I simply say, "pray for me, pray for me."

### A Smile on my Face, and a Joke in my Mouth

A Smile on My Face, and a Joke in My Mouth really opens
up the core of my feelings which can't be hidden. I tell
people a joke when I talk to them – they say, "Laughter is
the best medicine." This page begins negative but as you
see when you come to the end, I'm more on a positive note.
I think we all have down sides at times – it's who we are.
Still we try to let others know that in spite of how down we
are, we try to keep smiling.

## A Smile on my Face, and a Joke in my Mouth

I can't handle it Lord and I don't know what to do. I'm so tired right now, but I still want to wait until I see you. I'm trying to get my book together, "I'll Meet You on the Other Side. "I'm just putting it in folders for now. I'd rather have a finished book, but that's my pride.

I know I need to work on that Lord and so many other faults I have. I try, Lord. I really try, but I need to try harder. I forced myself to stay awake this morning so I could work on what needs to be done, but I'm giving in now – I'm such a hopeless one. But I'm tired and I'm worn out and I just don't feel good. Perhaps a nap will help, but my naps seem to go on and on.

There is so much more I want to do before I leave my dwelling place. I want to write words or tape them to my friends and loved ones, to tell them how much they have meant to me as the years have gone by. And I want to write more to help them to know and love You as I do.

I want You to fill me with Your words that will help people get through the days and years. To let them know everything will be all right even though they shed many, many tears.

Help me be a good person, Lord, and show me what to do to make You proud of me as I travel this life through. Through all the pain and suffering, I really don't mind, it Lord. You suffered so much for me. But it is hard, Lord. So very hard, yet others have it worse. Put a smile on my face

and a joke in my mouth so I can make others laugh and see
that with trust in You, they will be all right.

## The Lady in the Mirror

The Lady in the Mirror shows what I see in the mirror –
some of you may know what I am talking about; others
may not have seen this in their mirror.

## The Lady in the Mirror

I look at the face in the mirror
And I see a lady dying.
To see a once vibrant woman
Is the reason for my crying.

I've seen that look before
On my Dad and on my brother.
The eyes look sad and weak
But I don't remember that look on my mother.

Some days I look better
And think I can live forever,
But my earthly eyes tell me it's not true
They are sad and withdrawn and oh so blue.

The circle of life goes on and on,
A new baby born and an old one is gone.
The older you get, time moves fast.
I wonder which breath will be my last.

So many dreams have come and gone.

I've accomplished a lot, now it is time to move on.
I thank the Lord for all He has given me
My wonderful friends and my family.

## Light at the End of the Tunnel

Light at the End of the Tunnel talks about my deepest fear
– getting Dementia or Alzheimer's. This illness is so hard
on loved ones – especially when your parent or whoever
you care about doesn't recognize you anymore. This poem
I wrote about five years ago – it seemed to fit in my
writings. This is the only poem in my book that wasn't
written at the time the other ones were.

## Light at the End of the Tunnel

For so long the way was dark –
  Despair totally consumed me.
I shouted to the Lord and to all who would hear
  To just let me be.

But the Lord never gives up –
  Especially on those in despair.
He knows how you feel – your pain and your grief
  And He knows how much you can bear.

I asked so many times for His suffering.
  Now I know you can't understand why
I wanted to take pain from those who could take no more
  And wished that they could die.

The physical pain is fine with me –

I don't ask that He take it away.
But when I thought I was losing my mind
  I asked the Lord to help me find a way.

To be able to understand is
  One of God's greatest gifts.
Without it we can't help others
  And loved ones are especially missed.

He has His purpose – He has His reasons -
  Although many a time we don't understand why.
Why women, men, and children around Him
  Have to suffer and painfully die.

I cried and I pleaded
  To put my mind back on track.
And help me to deal with
  The mind that I lacked.

And suddenly one night I saw the light
  At the end of the tunnel so bright.
At last! At last there was hope
  All ablaze in the bright light.

I knew I could go on – there was hope for me.
  From insanity I was finally free –
God still has plans for the one He loves,
  And I thank God the Father, and Son from above.

## His Voice

I end my book with His Voice. God is calling me, but He is letting me put my affairs in order.

## His Voice

I can hear His gentle call.
I know, though, that He is not ready for me yet.
There is more on earth He wants me to do.

I listen carefully for His precious voice
To let me know how I can still
Serve Him here on earth.

There is so much He would have me do
And so little time to get it done.

These are earthly hours and earthly days -
A lot different than when you go to Heaven
And live eternally by His side.

I can hardly wait for Him
When on that holy day
He takes me up beside Him
And takes away my worries, tears, and pain.

Oh, the honor and the privilege
Of standing oh so near
To the one who really loves me
And takes me as I am.

## NOTES FROM THE AUTHOR:

I hope this book has been of some help to you. May it touch your heart as it has mine. As you journeyed through this book, my wish is that you found comfort and peace and answers to some of your questions. May you find the warmth of God's love and the knowledge you seek.

Believe there are others who feel the same as you. Some day it will all become clear, but in the meantime knowing God's love surrounds us as He holds us, cares for us and is willing to forgive all of our faults if we ask Him.

May you be at peace.
Mary Rita WaldschmidtBauck